Heinrich Preschers

**Letter from the Secretary of War**

Heinrich Preschers

**Letter from the Secretary of War**

ISBN/EAN: 9783744657211

Printed in Europe, USA, Canada, Australia, Japan

Cover: Foto ©ninafisch / pixelio.de

More available books at **www.hansebooks.com**

## TUNNELING DETROIT RIVER.

---

# LETTER

FROM

# THE SECRETARY OF WAR,

TRANSMITTING,

*With a letter from the Chief of Engineers, a report of a Board of Engineers on the practicability and approximate cost of tunneling the Detroit River, at or near Detroit, Mich., in compliance with the joint resolution of April 19, 1890.*

---

MAY 8, 1890.—Referred to the Committee on Rivers and Harbors.

---

WAR DEPARTMENT,
*Washington City, May 7, 1890.*

The Secretary of War has the honor to transmit to the House of Representatives a letter from the Chief of Engineers, dated the 6th instant, submitting a copy of the report of a Board of Engineers and its accompanying papers, on the practicability and approximate cost of tunneling the Detroit River at or near Detroit, Mich., in compliance with the provisions of joint resolution approved April 19, 1890.

REDFIELD PROCTOR,
*Secretary of War.*

The SPEAKER OF THE HOUSE OF REPRESENTATIVES.

---

OFFICE OF THE CHIEF OF ENGINEERS,
UNITED STATES ARMY,
*Washington, D. C., May 6, 1890.*

SIR: For the purpose of complying with the provisions of the joint resolution approved April 19, 1890, the Board of Engineers, constituted by Special Orders, No. 15 Headquarters, Corps of Engineers, February 8, 1889, to investigate and report upon the practicability and necessity of a bridge across the Detroit River at Detroit, Mich., was, by direction of the Secretary of War, reconvened by Special Orders, No. 21, Headquarters, Corps of Engineers, dated April 21, 1890, to consider and report upon public resolution, approved April 19, 1890, "Requesting the Secretary of War to cause a further report to be made as to the practicability and approximate cost of tunneling the Detroit River, at or near Detroit, Mich."

The report of the Board, dated May 3, 1890, has just reached this office, and a copy, with its accompanying papers, is submitted herewith, from which it will be seen that in the opinion of the Board the construction of the tunnel is practicable at an estimated cost of $3,500,000 (exclusive of land damages) for a single-track railway, and that there is no objection to authorizing its construction under the bed of the river.

Very respectfully, your obedient servant,

THOS. LINCOLN CASEY,
*Brig. Gen., Chief of Engineers.*

Hon. REDFIELD PROCTOR,
*Secretary of War.*

---

REPORT OF BOARD OF ENGINEERS ON TUNNELING DETROIT RIVER.

UNITED STATES ENGINEER OFFICE,
*Detroit, Mich., May 3, 1890.*

SIR: Complying with the provisions of joint resolution of Congress approved April 19, 1890, the Board of Engineers convened by Special Orders, No. 21, Headquarters, Corps of Engineers, April 21, 1890, has the honor to submit the following report:

The Board met at Detroit, Mich., April 30, 1890, at 10 a. m., all the members being present. The following instructions were read, viz:

OFFICE OF THE CHIEF OF ENGINEERS,
UNITED STATES ARMY,
*Washington, D. C., April 23, 1890.*

COLONEL: The accompanying copy of public resolution No. 14, entitled, "Joint resolution requesting the Secretary of War to cause a further report to be made as to the practicability and approximate cost of tunneling the Detroit River at or near Detroit, Mich.," approved April 19, 1890, is furnished for information of, and consideration by, the Board of Engineers constituted by Special Orders, No. 21, Headquarters, Corps of Engineers, April 21, 1890, of which you are the senior member.

The duties of the Board and the information desired are so clearly stated in the resolution that no supplementary instructions by this office are deemed necessary.

By command of Brig. Gen. Casey:
Very respectfully, your obedient servant,

THOS. TURTLE,
*Captain, Corps of Engineers.*

Col. O. M. POE,
*Corps of Engineers.*

[Public resolution No. 14.]

JOINT RESOLUTION requesting the Secretary of War to cause a further report to be made as to the practicability and approximate cost of tunneling the Detroit River, at or near Detroit, Michigan.

Whereas there having been commissions of Army engineers appointed in the years eighteen hundred and seventy-three, eighteen hundred and seventy-nine, and eighteen hundred and eighty-nine to investigate and report upon the necessity and practicability of the proper means of crossing the Detroit River, at or near Detroit, Michigan, by bridge or otherwise, and

Whereas said commissioners have limited such investigations more particularly to the question of bridging said river: Therefore,

*Resolved by the Senate and House of Representatives of the United States of America in Congress assembled,* That the Secretary of War is hereby directed to have the said Board of Engineers appointed by the Secretary of War in 1889 to more fully report upon (at the earliest time practicable) the advisability, practicability, and approximate cost of tunneling the Detroit River, at or near Detroit, Mich., in such a manner as to accommodate the large trade and commerce crossing the river at that point without permanent obstruction of any kind whatever to the navigation interests of

said river, with a view to the passage of said commerce through said tunnel from the
United States into and through the Dominion of Canada, and return; such report to
be based upon the examination already made by said Board, or, if necessary to a compliance with this resolution, to make such report after further inquiry into the
subject.

Approved April 19, 1890.

The duties of the Board appear to be comprehended in the require-
ment that they shall report upon

The advisability, practicability, and approximate cost of tunneling Detroit River,
at or near Detroit, Mich., in such manner as to accommodate the large trade and
commerce crossing the river at that point, without permanent obstruction of any
kind whatever to the navigation interests of said river.

The Board remained in session four days, devoting two days to listen-
ing to such persons as desired to furnish information or present their
views upon the subject.

Mr. Luther Beecher and Dr. Sherman appeared before the Board
and explained their respective plans for constructing a tunnel under
Detroit River, and Mr. L. Grover partly explained a method of his own
for what he styled shallow tunneling, though he presented no plans or
models.

Two copies of Mr. Beecher's patents are herewith marked A and B.

A communication, with blue prints, from U. S. G. White, Civil Engineer, U. S. Navy, was received. A circular from Mr. Charles H.
Buckelew, explaining his proposed method of tunneling, and a letter
from Mr. R. P. Rothwell, inviting attention to the Hall method of tunneling, were also received. These papers are herewith marked C, D,
E, and F.

The Board personally examined a tunnel for a single-track railroad
now in progress under St. Clair River at Port Huron, Mich., which,
when completed, will be about 6,100 feet long, a part of the tunnel being under the river banks. The width of the river at this point is
2,300 feet, and the tunnel work has been advanced 200 feet under it on
the Michigan side and has reached a point 100 feet short of the bank of
the river on the Canada side. The tunnel is being pushed forward at the
rate of 16 to 20 feet a day, 8 to 10 feet on each side of the river, and it is
expected that it will be completed in six months. It seems probable that
it will be opened for traffic in 1891. The estimated cost of this work,
as published in a technical journal is $2,500,000. The material through
which a tunnel under Detroit River, at Detroit, would have to be constructed, is similar to that through which the St. Clair River tunnel.
is now being successfully pushed forward toward completion.

Taking up the subjects for report, as required by the joint resolution,
in their order, the first that presents itself is that of the advisability of
tunneling Detroit River at or near Detroit. The advisability of select-
ing any particular mode of crossing the river depends very largely upon
the amount and character of the traffic to be provided for, coupled
with the comparative cost of crossing by different modes having sufficient capacity to pass the traffic.

It is stated in the report of this Board dated July 19, 1889, that
389,239 cars were transported across the river by ferry in 1887, and
374,426 in 1888, or an average of more than 1,000 cars per day. The
reasons advanced for the necessity of some crossing other than by ferry
are also stated in that report, so that it is not necessary to dwell upon
that question in this paper.

As railroad traffic across the Detroit River increases, the disadvan-
tages of the ferriage system will increase.

The erection of any bridge across the Detroit River will always be more or less objectionable to navigation interests, and even if a high bridge were unobjectionable, its cost, including approaches, would undoubtedly be in excess of the cost of two single-track tunnels.

So far as the interests of navigation are considered, the construction of a tunnel would undoubtedly be advisable, but whether it would be correspondingly advantageous to the railroad interests will depend on the cost of a tunnel.

The Board is of the opinion that there is no objection to the author- ization by Congress of the construction of a tunnel under the bed of the river, but at no point with less than 30 feet of water over its top, by any railroad or corporation interested. All railroads should be per- mitted to pass cars through the tunnel on payment of a reasonable and fixed charge to be determined by the Secretary of War.

In regard to the practicability of making a tunnel under the Detroit River the Board is of the opinion that the recent progress made in the construction of subaqueous tunnels through difficult materials in Eng- land, under the Hudson at New York, and under St. Clair River at Port Huron, demonstrates the practicability of constructing a tunnel at Detroit where the material through which a tunnel is proposed is not believed to be more difficult than that at Port Huron.

And it is the further opinion of the Board that $3,500,000 will cover the cost of a tunnel for a single-track railway under Detroit River. This estimate includes the cost of approaches, but not the cost of land damages, which will depend upon the location of the tunnel.

All of which is respectfully submitted.

O. M. POE,
*Colonel, Corps of Engineers, etc.*
CHAS. J. ALLEN,
*Major, Corps of Engineers.*
H. M. ADAMS,
*Major, Corps of Engineers.*

Brig. Gen. THOMAS L. CASEY,
*Chief of Engineers, U. S. Army.*

---

LETTER OF THE DETROIT RAILROAD AND TUNNEL COMPANY.

DETROIT, MICH., *April* 29, 1890.

DEAR SIR: The Detroit Railroad and Tunnel Company, a responsible corporation, organized under the laws of the State of Michigan, is prepared to enter into contract with any responsible parties for the construction of a tunnel under the Detroit River at or near Detroit, and its approaches, for the passage of railroad trains, upon the following terms: Upon the basis of 3,000 feet of tunnel and 6,000 feet of approaches; the tunnel, under the river and for 100 feet on the natural bank of the river on each side, to consist of a solid combined cast-iron tube, 20 feet in diameter in the clear, from 5 to 12 inches thick, its top to be at least 30 feet below low-water mark; the approaches to said tunnel to be so constructed as to secure a grade not exceeding 80 feet to the mile, to be built of timber, stone, and brick and cement masonry 3 feet thick for a distance of 500 feet from the tunnel, 2½ feet for the next 500 feet, and 2 feet thick, or an open cut, for the remaining distance; to be 20 feet in diameter in the clear, the whole to be finished complete and ready for use within two years from the date of contract. The parties of the other part furnishing the necessary charters from the United States and Canadian Governments, and also the necessary right of way and grounds required for the storage of material and the carrying on of the work. The whole to be constructed and finished complete for use with all necessary permanent works to provide proper drainage and ventilation for the sum of $3,500,000, or two tunnels alongside each other for $6,500,000. Said tunnel to be built under the patents issued by the United States and Canada to Luther Beecher for device and improvement in the method of constructing, and constructed, subaqueous tunnels, hereto attached

THE DETROIT RAILROAD AND TUNNEL CO.,
LUTHER BEECHER,
*President.*
S. S. TROWBRIDGE,
*Director.*

General O. M. POE,
*Chairman, Board of Engineers.*

----

## A.

[United States Patent Office. Luther Beecher, of Detroit, Michigan. Specification forming part of Letters Patent No. 413384, dated October 22, 1889. Application filed March 5, 1889. Serial No. 302026. No model.]

### TUNNELING-RAM.

*To all whom it may concern:*

Be it known that I, Luther Beecher, a citizen of the United States, residing at Detroit, in the county of Wayne and State of Michigan, have invented certain new and useful improvements in tunneling-rams, of which the following is a specification, reference being had therein to the accompanying drawings.

This invention relates to new and useful improvements in the art of constructing subaqueous tunnels; and the invention primarily consists in the mechanical means and appliances by which I intend to carry out a method of tunneling, for which I have concurrently applied for letters patent; and it further consists in the peculiar construction of the tunneling-casing, all as more fully hereinafter described, and shown in the accompanying drawings.

My method of tunneling contemplates the construction of subaqueous tunnels without the necessity of removing the earth, as in the present methods of constructing such tunnels. To this end the way for the tunnel-casing is forced by means of a wedge-shaped bulk-head, or what I call a "tunneling-ram," which slides with a water-tight joint on the construction end of the tunnel-casing, and which is driven forward with sufficient power to displace the earth in front of it upwardly, so as to cover the top of the tunnel, the latter passing in suitable proximity to and below the bottom of a river or body of water to permit this displacement of the earth. To assist the operation of the tunneling-ram the earth in front of it, if necessary, is loosened up to the required depth, and stones, rocks, or other obstacles are removed or broken up by the use of explosives. This work is accomplished with the help of a vessel provided with the required outfit and operating in advance of the tunneling-ram. Plastic packing is used to form a water-tight joint between the casing and the sliding end of the tunneling-ram, and this packing remains permanently on the outside of the casing.

Devises are provided for steering the tunneling-ram and other provisions are made to meet contingencies necessitating the temporary use of other modes of tunneling.

In the drawings, Figure 1 is a vertical cross-section of a tunnel in process of construction in accordance with my invention. Fig. 2 is an enlarged vertical central longitudinal section of the construction end thereof. Fig. 3 is a cross-section of the tunnel as completed. Fig. 4 is a cross-section of the tunneling-ram on line X X of Fig. 2. Fig. 5 is a plan thereof. Fig. 6 is an enlarged perspective view of a plate of the casting of which I intend to construct my tunnel. Fig. 7 is a cross-section on line Y Y of Fig. 2; and Fig. 8 is a detail cross-section through two plates, showing the construction of the joints.

A are segmental rectangular plates of cast-iron, smooth on the outside and provided on the edges with inwardly projecting flanges *a* for bolting the plates endwise and sidewise together to form a tunnel of the desired cross-section. Similar flanges or ribs *b* may be provided centrally to strengthen the plates.

To form water-tight joints I provide all the plates alike upon their ends and sides with tenons *c* and grooves *d*, whereby in joining the plates together the tenons on one plate will engage into the corresponding grooves in the adjoining plates. The plates are preferably bolted together to break joints, and soft metal gaskets B are inserted between the joints. For the purpose I use, preferably, lead plates, through which the bolt-holes are formed by means of a pointed tool, which gradually enlarges the bolt-hole to force the lead into the joint between the flanges around the bolt-hole. In addition to this metallic packing, the joints may be coated with paint, asphalt, coal-tar, or any other compound usually used in constructions of this kind. These metallic plates I make of a size and shape convenient for handling and to be readily transported through the interior of the tunnel as its construction advances.

I deem cast-iron to be the most suitable material for constructing the plates; but I do not intend to limit myself to this material alone, or to its exclusive use, for if occasion should require or I should deem it expedient I intend to provide the casing with a suitable lining on the inside—such as masonry, terra cotta, cement, or other heavy material—or fill the openings formed between the flanges of each plate with solid cast-iron blocks, firmly wedged or keyed in as may be required to give the necessary strength, weight, and stability to the structure and to overcome the buoyancy thereof and the pressure of water upon it.

While building this tunnel on land I proceed, as usual, by excavating the earth, and in lengthening the tunnel I add the sections on top first to form a protecting-hood, and gradually add plates to the sides and bottom, keeping the top plates always advanced. In building this tunnel under the bed of a river, lake, etc., I proceed after the method described above, by building on the open end of the tunnel-casing the hollow sliding bulk-head or tunneling-ram C, which is wedge-shaped at its forward end and slightly tapering at its rear end and sufficiently larger than the tunnel to loosely embrace it and form an annular space for packing. This tunneling-ram I construct in a similar manner of sectional plates, as described for the casing of the tunnel, except that the tapering end is smooth on the inside. The front edge or wedge-shaped portion I construct, preferably, in a solid manner, and with a movable point or nose D, which is connected by a strong knuckle-joint, which turns on the steel shaft E, and is solidly backed in circular bearings on the head. This movable nose is adapted to be raised or lowered by providing it with hydraulic chambers e and f, or with suitable mechanical devices—such as the lever g—adapted to be worked from the inside and having a sufficient amplitude of motion to raise or lower the point within the easy grades permissible for tunnels. The whole point or wedge-shaped portion of the tunneling-ram is solidly constructed of cast-iron or steel to resist the hydraulic pressure exerted against it by a series of hydraulic cylinders F, placed against its bulk-head and disposed near the outside of the shell, and forming a strengthening part thereto, and being integral therewith or forming an inner lining therefor. The pistons G of these hydraulic cylinders, which correspond in number with the number of plates composing the circle, operate in the longitudinal direction of the ram, and are in a line corresponding with the casing of the tunnel, whereby in operation the force of the piston may be exerted endwise and in a line with the casing or wall of the tunnel, each piston being suitably blocked or abutted against the contiguous portion of the casing or walls of the tunnel to exert a direct thrust upon it when the hydraulic pressure is exerted upon the piston. The hydraulic pressure can be applied for two purposes—first, for forcing the tunneling-ram the necessary distance ahead to lengthen the tunnel-casing, and secondly, to force each individual plate into position when the tunnel is lengthened out, as it requires some power to compress the packing sufficiently to make the tongue-and-groove joints with the soft-metal packing between, as described. By constructing the pistons with the screw-extension G', as shown, they may be readily abutted against the plates. When hydraulic pressure is applied to all the pistons to drive the tunneling-ram the necessary distance forward, all the plates will be firmly compacted endwise and sidewise; also, on account of the pressure on the casting and of the slightly tapering shape of the tunneling-ram, the bolts are uniformly tightened on all the joints wherever necessary.

To form a tight joint between the overlapping ends of the tunneling-ram and the casing of the tunnel I compact into the annular space a plastic packing or cement, preferably composed of asphalt, coal-tar, or other bitumen mixed with cement and with a fibrous material—such as tow or old rope—and this packing is of an adhesive nature and hardens and sets after a while. As the tunneling-ram advances by being forced forward, the packing is compressed onto the casing by the tapering rear end, and is thereby forced into all the joints of the casing and forms an outer protective layer around the tunnel. New packing is added whenever the casing is lengthened out.

As my method of tunneling contemplates the building of the tunnel just below the bottom of the body of water as nearly as is possible without making too many or abrupt changes in the grade of the tunnel, I raise or lower the hinged nose of the tunneling-ram in a proper degree to steer the tunneling-ram up or down, as required. The power of the hydraulic pistons may also be applied to effect the steering of the tunneling-ram up or down or to one side or the other by applying the pressure unequally to the bulk-head.

To effect the lateral steering of the tunneling-ram by mechanical means I provide the latter, near the forward end, with the hinged wings H, which fold into suitable recesses provided upon the side of the tunneling-ram and are provided with hydraulic pressure chambers or other mechanical devices to open them laterally when required to crowd the tunneling-ram to one side or the other.

The advantage obtained by keeping always in the same proximity below the bed of the river or other body of water, or nearly so, is that I thereby make it possible for my tunneling-ram to displace the ground in front thereof upwardly when forced ahead by suitable hydraulic pressure. At the same time the ground is firmly compacted all around and forms a protective layer over the top of the tunnel, which is composed of the solid soil raised up from the bottom of the tunnel, and which may be afterward further compacted from the outside in any suitable manner. The light material—such as silt and other débris usually found on the bottom of rivers, etc.—is raised up from the bottom to be carried away by the water.

My method of tunneling in close proximity to the bottom of the water permits me to simultaneously carry on the operation of loosening the soil in advance of the tunneling-ram. This I carry out by anchoring a suitable scow, boat, or raft I in advance of the tunneling-ram, which is provided with suitable mechanical devices to loosen, work, or puddle the ground in advance of the ram from above, such as by means of suitable tools lowered into the ground to the required depth. By this operation I also discover any obstacles to the progress of the tunneling-ram, and remove the same in any suitable manner, such as by means of explosives or otherwise. This operation of loosening the soil in advance of the tunneling-ram may be entirely accomplished, if desired, by the use of explosives, as in the usual operation of deepening channel-beds in rock-bottom. By loosening and working the ground in this manner not only bowlders and other obstacles are discovered, but the work of the tunneling-ram becomes at once possible under all conditions of soil, and, as clayey soil is thereby transformed into a plastic cement, a new element of strength and durability is added to the structure, as the clay, after becoming compacted again, forms a water-proof covering around the tunnel.

For such contingencies as are found in subaqueous constructions, where liability exists from being undermined, as where channels are changing, I introduce a new element of protection, which consists of driving piles alongside the casing of the tunnel, slightly inclined, so as to pin or hold the tunnel to the bed, and placed in pairs opposite to each other to permit of their being yoked together over the top of the tunnel by suitable cross-pieces or iron yokes. This piling may be carried out in advance of the tunnel to guide the tunneling-ram in its operation, in which case the side wings for steering are not required.

In the practical construction of my tunnel, I start the subaqueous portion of the tunnel preferably from the bottom of a vertical shaft of suitable size to afford a convenient entrance into the tunnel for lowering the material, and serving also as an air-shaft. On the bottom of this shaft I provide a cistern or well suitable to receive the ordinary leakage or drainage from the tunnel, and from which it may be pumped out. This I cover over with a strong platform in line with the bottom of the intended tunnel, and upon this I begin to construct my tunneling-ram, projecting out through the sides of the shaft. If necessary, a suitable coffer is constructed outside around the tunneling-ram to protect the shaft against the ingress of water. After the tunneling-ram is completed I begin to construct a section of my tunnel-casing inside of the rear end of the tunneling-ram, and after securing the packing in place the rear end of the casing is abutted against the rear side of the shaft, and the front end of each plate of the casing I abut against its corresponding hydraulic piston. After having made all the necessary provisions for allowing the tunneling-ram to be pushed ahead in the manner intended, this operation is then proceeded with by forcing water by means of a large force-pump—preferably placed in proximity to the shaft—into the hydraulic cylinders until the tunneling-ram has advanced the necessary distance required for securing new plates to the tunnel-casing after the pistons are withdrawn into the hydraulic cylinders. By alternatingly driving the tunneling-ram ahead and lengthening the casing, adding to it a new set of plates all around with the necessary packing to maintain a water-tight joint, the construction of the tunnel is carried out substantially after the method described.

It is obvious that I intend to avail myself of all the facilities and modern appliances of which engineers in carrying out such construction generally avail themselves —such as laying a temporary track inside the tunnel, for running a train or trucks thereon to transport the material, the construction of suitable drains and pipe systems to afford drainage, and to convey the hydraulic pressure into the hydraulic cylinders, and other suitable provisions for lighting, heating, or whatever may be required for the comfort of the workmen and for expediting the work.

There may be sections of work where my method of tunneling is not available or would be at a disadvantage compared with other known methods; but it will be an easy matter to make suitable provisions in the construction of the tunneling-ram to permit of using excavating machinery applied through suitable openings provided for in the bulk-head. As the nature of the work and the difficulties to be encountered can all be known in advance through a careful survey, which ought necessarily to precede the commencement of the work, no contingencies are liable to arrive for which no adequate provisions can be made or which engineering skill is not able to meet, and while quicksand is generally accounted to be the most troublesome factor in tunnel construction no difficulty at all arises from this source in my method of tunneling.

No claim is made to the process herein described, as it forms the subject-matter of my application, Serial No. 298,183, filed January 31, 1889.

What I claim as my invention is—

1. In subaqueous tunneling, a tunneling-ram provided with a wedge-shaped bulk-head adapted to displace the ground upwardly, having a hinged point or nose and forming a water-tight compartment slidingly operating on the head of the tunnel-casing, substantially as described.

2. In subaqueous tunneling, a tunneling-ram provided with a solid bulk-head constructed in the form of a wedge, adapted to displace the ground upwardly when pushed through it, and with a movable point or nose for steering it, said tunneling-ram being adapted to slidingly operate on the head of the tunnel-casing, and forming a water-tight compartment for extending the tunnel-casing, within said tunneling-ram, substantially as described.

3. In subaqueous tunneling, a tunneling-ram provided at its front end with a solid bulk-head, having its front face rearwardly inclined from the bottom to the top and having a hinged point or nose and laterally-extensible wings, substantially as described.

4. The combination, with the casing and tunneling-ram slidingly secured thereon and formed with tapered rear end, of the plastic packing applied between the tunneling-ram and casing to form a water-tight joint, substantially as described.

5. In subaqueous tunneling, the combination, with the casing, of a tunneling-ram provided with a tapering rear end and a plastic packing applied in the annular space between said tapering rear end and the casing of the tunnel, said tunneling-ram forming a water-tight compartment on the head of the casing and provided with means for advancing it to permit of extending the casing within the tunneling-ram, substantially as described.

6. In subaqueous tunneling, the combination, with a casing constructed of rectangular segmental cast-iron plates smooth on the outside and interiorly flanged on their edges for securing said plates together by bolts of the tunneling-ram provided with a tapering rear end smooth on the inside and slidingly engaging with the end of the tunnel-casing by means of plastic packing adapted to form a permanent covering on the outside of the tunnel-casing, substantially as described.

7. In subaqueous tunneling, the combination of a tunnel-casing consisting of rectangular segmental iron plates adapted to be interiorly bolted together with intervening gaskets by means of interior flanges provided with corresponding tongues and grooves, a tunneling-ram provided with a solid bulk-head wedge-shaped at its outer face and with a tapering rear end sliding on the head of the casing, with a water-tight joint formed of a plastic material adapted to form a permanent covering on the outside of the tunnel-casing, and a series of hydraulic rams grouped around the inner wall of said tunneling-ram and adapted to operate with their pistons against the inner ends of the plates of the casing to force the same in place and advance the tunneling-ram, substantially as described.

In testimony whereof I affix my signature, in presence of two witnesses, this 22d day of December, 1888.

LUTHER BEECHER

Witnesses:
.   J. PAUL MAYER,
     P. M. HULBERT.

---

## B.

### METHOD OF CONSTRUCTING TUNNELS.

[United States Patent Office. Luther Beecher, of Detroit, Michigan. Specification forming part of Letters Patent No. 413,383, dated October 22, 1889. Application filed January 31, 1889. Serial No. 298,183. No model.]

*To all whom it may concern :*

Be it known that I, Luther Beecher, a citizen of the United States, residing at Detroit, in the county of Wayne and State of Michigan, have invented certain new and useful Improvements in the Method of Constructing Tunnels, of which the following is a specification, reference being had therein to the accompanying drawings.

This invention relates to new and useful improvements in the art of constructing subaqueous tunnels under rivers, lakes, harbors, inlets, marshes, and lowlands ; and the invention consists in the improved method of construction, whereby I am not

L. BEECHER.

TUNNELING RAM.

No. 413,384.                        Patented Oct. 22, 1889.

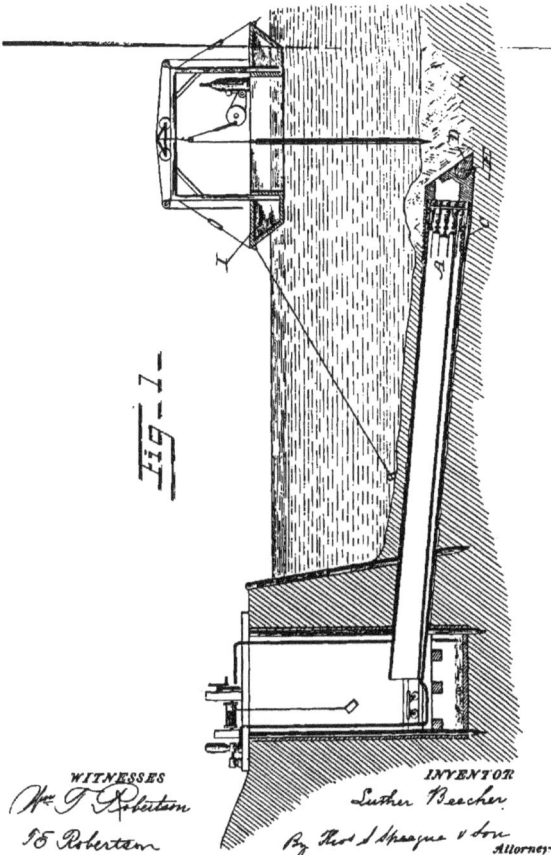

_Fig - 1_

L. BEECHER.
TUNNELING RAM.

No. 413,384.　　　　　　　　　Patented Oct. 22, 1889.

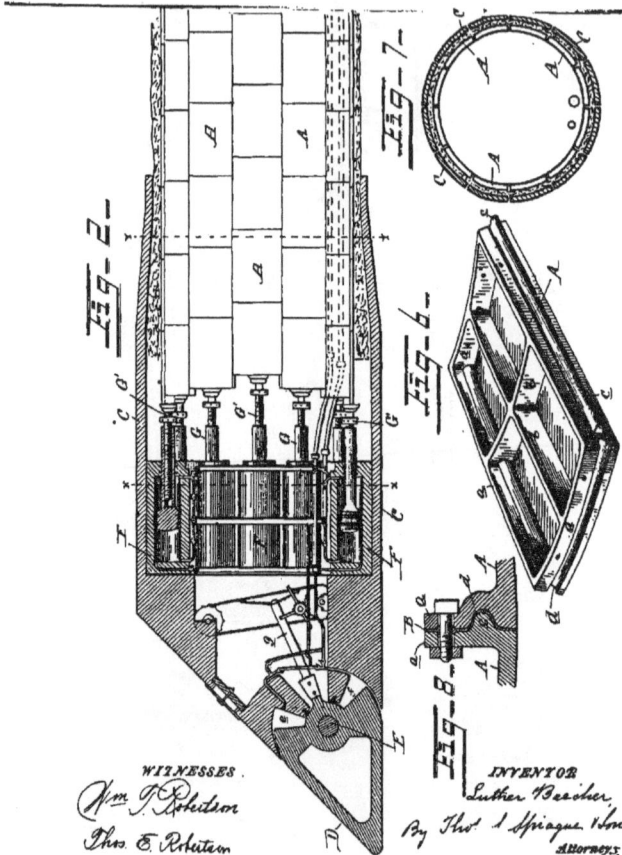

Fig-7-

Fig-2-

Fig-6-

Fig-8-

WITNESSES.
Wm J. Robertson
Thos. E. Robertson

INVENTOR
Luther Beecher
By Thos. J. Sprague & Son
Attorneys.

H Ex...3.6.9.....51 1

L. BEECHER.
TUNNELING RAM.

No. 413,384.          Patented Oct. 22, 1889.

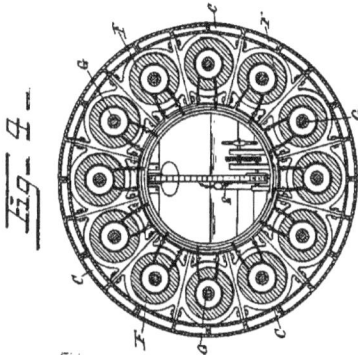

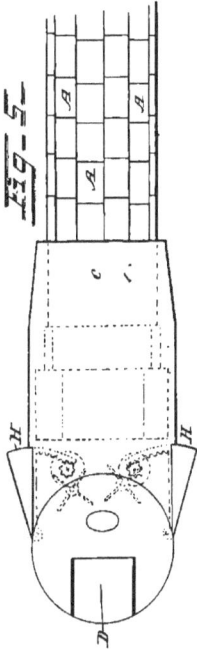

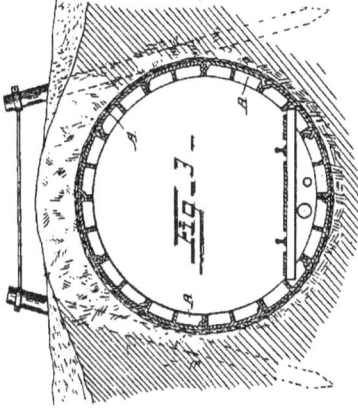

INVENTOR
Luther Beecher
By Thos S. Sprague & Son
Attorneys

H Ex 369.....51 1

only enabled to advance the tunnel without resorting to the necessity of excavating, boring, or removing the earth, as is the case with the methods in present use, but whereby the earth, instead of being removed, becomes in my construction an element of strength and protection to the tunnel, all as more fully hereinafter described, and set forth in the accompanying drawings, in which—

Figure 1 is a verticle cross-section through a river, illustrating the method of building my tunnel. Fig. 2 is an enlarged cross-section of the tunnel as completed. Fig. 3 is an enlarged longitudinal central section through a portion of the completed tunnel, with the tunneling-ram in position as in the act of operation. Fig. 4 is a perspective view of one of the plates of which I preferably construct the casing of the tunnel. Fig. 5 is a diagram plan view of the tunneling-ram, illustrating the devices for steering it. Fig. 6 is a cross-section on line X X in Fig. 3. Fig. 7 is a cross-section on line Y Y in Fig. 3. Fig. 8 is a detail cross-section through two plates, showing the construction of the joint.

A is the main casing of the tunnel. It may be of any desired cross-section, and is constructed of metal plates, preferably of rectangular cast-iron plates B, smooth upon the outside, and provided with inwardly-projecting flanges C, for securing the plates together on their edges by bolts. These plates are of suitable curvature to form, when secured together, the desired cross-section of the tunnel, and of a size not too large and heavy to be brought in through the completed portion of the tunnel-casing and to be readily secured from the inside. The plates are preferably made of even length and secured together to lap at the sides. To form water-tight joints, the plates are provided upon their edges with corresponding tongues and grooves, and gaskets are placed between the joints. For gaskets I choose lead plates perforated after the plates are jointed and ready to be bolted together by a pointed tool, which gradually enlarges a passage large enough for the bolt to pass through, whereby the the lead displaced is crowded into the joint around the bolt-hole and prevents leakage.

On the construction end of the tunnel I use the tunneling-ram C', which is of similar construction and cross-section as the tunnel, but suitably larger to form a sleeve on the casing of the tunnel. The forward end of this tunneling-ram is provided with a strong water-tight bulk-head D, the front face E of which is inclined from front to rear, substantially as shown. The rear end of the ram is slightly contracted or tapering, and is built smooth on the inside and forms an annular space for the packing F.

Within the tunneling-ram and abutting against the bulk-head are disposed a series of hydraulic cylinders G, the pistons H of which reciprocate in the axial line of the tunneling-ram, and these hydraulic cylinders are connected by pipes I with a suitable force-pump J or head, preferably located on the shore side of the tunnel in such manner as to operate the cylinders by hydraulic pressure in the well-known application of hydraulic jacks.

The nose or point K of the tunneling-ram is hinged in any suitable manner, and is provided with suitable steering-gear to raise or depress it, and hinged wings L are secured to the sides of the tunneling-ram in recesses formed therein, and provided with actuating-gear to be opened outwardly to any desired degree or secured in their recesses to be flush with the sides of the ram.

Having now described the elements of my improvement, I will proceed to describe the construction of a subaqueous tunnel in accordance with my method.

I first construct a suitable tunnel-shaft M in close proximity to the water, preferably near a dock or wharf, where the water has the average depth. On the bottom of this shaft, and projecting with its front portion through the wall of the shaft into a coffer formed by a temporary coffer-dam, I then construct the tunneling-ram at such a depth that when pushed ahead the tunneling-ram advances in solid ground. Within the rear end of the tunneling-ram, which projects inside the shaft, I then construct a section of the casing and firmly brace the same against the opposite wall of the shaft, providing ample space for unobstructed access into the tunnel. After securing a suitable packing in the annular space between the tapering rear end of the tunneling-ram and the casing, as hereinafter described, and abutting the ends of the pistons against the edge of the casing by the use of suitable blocking, sufficient hydraulic pressure is applied to the cylinders to push the tunneling-ram forward the necessary distance for adding new plates to the tunnel-casing. The travel of the pistons is made, preferably, equal to the length of the plates, and proper means are provided to withdraw the pistons into the cylinders after the operation of driving the tunneling-ram ahead is completed.

It is obvious that for subaqueous tunneling great care has to be taken to provide a reliable water-tight joint between the tunneling-ram and the casing of the tunnel. To this end I have devised a novel way of packing, which consists in stuffing into the annular space between the casing and the rear end of the tunneling-ram a plastic packing adapted to form a water-proof joint. Compositions of this kind are well known and used for various engineering purposes and may be readily adapted for to it and makes it water-proof, besides strengthening it and protecting it from rusting on the outside.

After the tunneling-ram is advanced by the application of sufficient hydraulic pressure into all the cylinders the pistons are retracted and a new set of plates with new packing are secured to the end of the casing. In this operation the hydraulic pressure from the cylinders may be individually applied to force each plate into position, and the plates are preferably only temporarily secured together until the joint hydraulic pressure from all the cylinders and the outside pressure have forced the plates into a permanent relation to each other.

The various details connected with these operations and not alluded to herein may be easily carried out by ordinary engineering skill, and obvious modifications of carrying out my method under different contingencies may be devised without departing from the spirit of my invention.

The best conditions for the application of my method of tunneling are found in ground reasonably free from rocks and obstructions and where the ground is for the most part so regular that the tunneling-ram can follow the same without producing too many or abrupt changes in the grade. By making preliminary surveys as required for the construction of any tunnel, no matter by what method, it will be generally found easy to select a suitable profile, especially by crossing under navigable rivers or bays.

My method of tunneling contemplates constructing the tunnel a few feet (more or less) below the bottom of the river, lake, or other body of water, to enable the ram to displace the earth in an upward direction into the water, and should abrupt change in the grade require it other known methods of tunneling may be temporarily applied to meet exceptional conditions. To this end suitable provision may be made in the construction of the tunneling-ram to permit of boring, drilling, excavating, or otherwise removing the earth, as may be determined in advance.

The conditions under which my method is applicable are those ordinarily found in crossing under rivers or lakes, in which there are generally a few inches or feet of loose sand, gravel, or silt on the bottom, with a solid bed of clay or clayey soil underneath. By advancing with the tunneling-ram in the solid bed the lighter particles are lifted above the bottom and gradually washed away, while the clay or heavy soil is compacted all around the tunnel and the portion displaced upwardly is left over the top of the tunnel to form a covering, which may be rammed down from above, and which, if of a clayey nature, may become of itself a water-tight medium around the tunnel. If desired or necessary on account of insufficient covering, suitable ballast may be thrown over the tunnel from the outside.

By using the steering-gear of the ram in a proper manner it will not be found difficult to follow the rise and fall of the bottom within the allowable limits; but if the means for steering should be inadaptable or inadequate, piles P may be driven at suitable intervals into the bed, preferably in pairs, far enough apart to let the tunneling-ram pass between and serve as guides. By connecting the upper end of each pair of piles with the yoke R the casing may be firmly anchored in place, if necessary, to prevent possible displacement.

The buoyancy of the tunnel and the tunneling-ram is counteracted by the use of cast-iron or other metal in the construction of all the parts, and, if need be, ballast inside applied as a lining to the tunnel-casing, or by securing cast-iron blocks into the panels formed between the flanges of the plates of the casing.

An important adjunct of my improvement is the operation of exploring the ground in advance of the tunneling-ram. This operation is intended for the purpose of discovering bowlders, rock, or other obstructions of a nature liable to form an obstacle to the tunneling, and also for the purpose of loosening and preparing the ground in advance of the head of the tunneling-ram, so that it will offer less resistance to displacement by the tunneling-ram and become of a more plastic nature, so as to pack around the tunnel. In clayey soil it is of especial value to loosen the soil, as it is well known that by a certain amount of working or so-called "puddling" it becomes quite plastic, and then forms an excellent covering or packing around the tunnel, which of itself is water-tight. This exploring or working of the ground is easily produced or effected by the use of a suitable vessel—such as a large scow—anchored in front of the tunneling-ram, and operating in the ground with suitable tools—such as heavy spuds—working up and down in the necessary manner to find all rocks and bowlders, or other obstructions, which are removed in any suitable manner.

Instead of loosening the ground with tools, the more modern way of using explo-

# L. BEECHER.
## METHOD OF CONSTRUCTING TUNNELS.

No. 413,383.                          Patented Oct. 22, 1889.

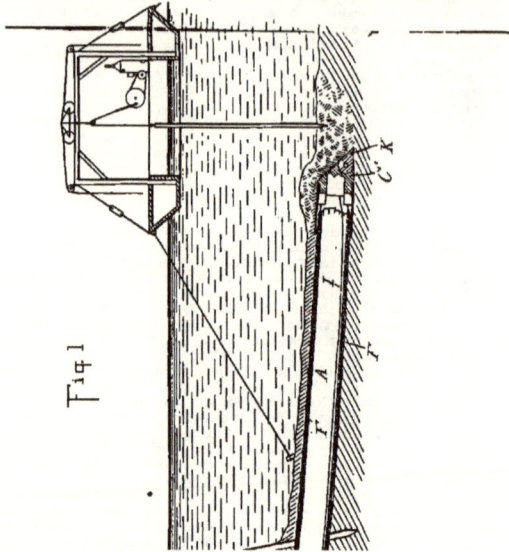

Fig 1

# L. BEECHER.
## METHOD OF CONSTRUCTING TUNNELS.

No. 413,383.                          Patented Oct. 22, 1889.

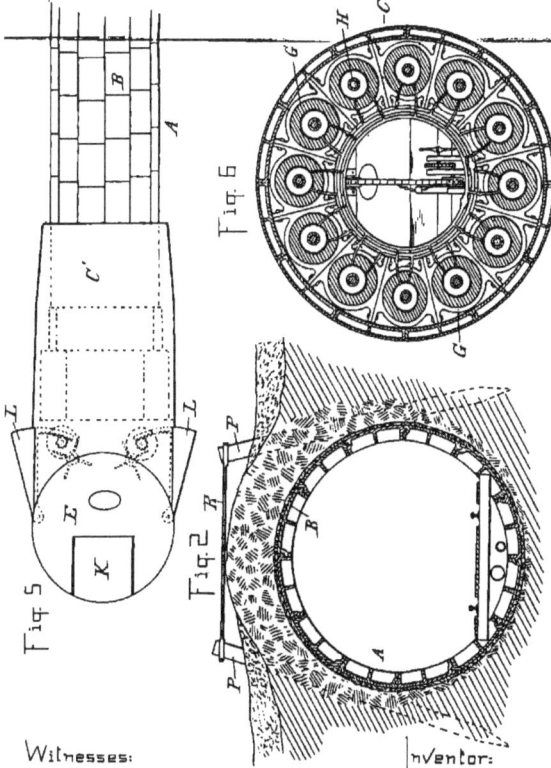

Fig. 6

Fig. 5

Fig. 2

H Ex. 369. 51 1

# L. BEECHER.
## METHOD OF CONSTRUCTING TUNNELS.

No. 413,383.        Patented Oct. 22, 1889.

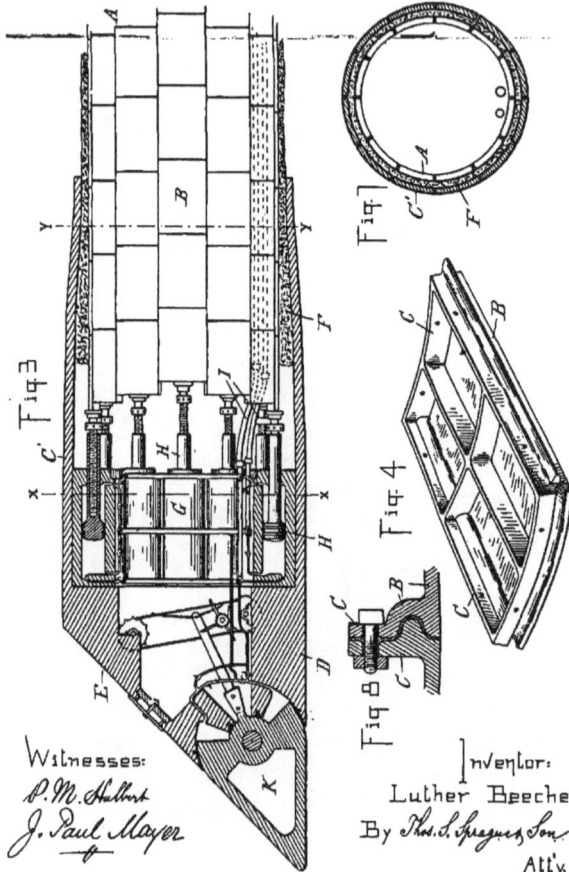

Witnesses:

P. M. Hulbert

J. Paul Mayer

Inventor:

Luther Beecher

By Thos. L. Sprague & Son,

Att'y.

H Ex 369 51 1

sives may bo made use of, which would also dispose of rocks or other obstructions. The manner of using dynamite or other explosives for similar purposes is so well known that a further description thereof may properly be omitted and left to the practical engineer.

It is obvious that although the material may be thoroughly loosened and worked up in advance of the tunneling-ram, and that it may be lifted up by the wedge-shaped end of the tunneling-ram, it will nevertheless again be firmly compacted upon the sides and top as the ram advances. Care should be taken, however, to loosen the soil not more than is needed to advance the tunneling-ram, and, if necessary, the loosened ground may be packed again afterward on top and on the sides of the tunnel-casing by the application of mechanical means.

As the presence of quicksands in the strata or in pockets does not in the least interfere with the successful operation of my method, the latter presents the most economical solution, not only of one of the most difficult engineering problems in tunneling, but in all subsequent tunnel constructions in which my method is applicable on general conditions.

The construction of my tunneling-ram in respect to the hinged nose or point and the hinged wings on the side is devised for the purpose of having it entirely within my power to direct or steer the tunneling-ram within a permissible limit up or down, right or left. The raising and lowering of the nose of the tunneling-ram will evidently direct the ram up or down in the same manner, and the spreading or folding of the lateral wings will cause a lateral deflection of the tunneling-ram to one side or the other, as desired, and as a further means of guiding the tunneling-ram in the intended direction a judicious use of the hydraulic jacks in the tunneling-ram forms another means of accomplishing this end.

I attach importance to the fact that the forward end of the ram be upon an incline, as shown, in contradistinction to being concaved or tapered from the longitudinal center to the sides, as heretofore, so that the earth is displaced upward and compressed above the casing instead of being thrown mostly to the sides and there compressed.

No claim is here made to the apparatus shown herein, as it forms the subject-matter of my application, Serial No. 302026, filed March 5, 1889.

What I claim as my invention is—

1. The herein-described improvement in the art of subaqueous tunnel construction, which consists in slidingly operating the tunneling-ram on the construction end of the tunnel-casing, and displacing the earth upward and extending the tunnel-casing step by step as the tunneling advances, and loosening or preparing the ground in advance of the ram by mechanical means removed from the ram as set forth.

2. The herein-described improvement in the art of subaqueous tunnel construction, which consists in slidingly operating the tunneling-ram on the construction end of the tunnel-casing and in compressing in a tapering space between the ram and the casing an outer covering in the advancing movement of the ram, as set forth.

3. The herein-described improvement in the art of subaqueous tunnel construction, which consists in extending the casing step by step within the tunneling-ram moving over said casing and compressing suitable packing in a tapering space between the casing and the ram and into the joints of the casing by the advancing movement of the ram, as set forth.

In testimony whereof I affix my signature in presence of two witnesses, this 22d day of December, 1888.

LUTHER BEECHER.

Witnesses :
J. PAUL MAYER,
P. M. HULBERT.

## C.

### LETTER OF MR. U. S. G. WHITE, CIVIL ENGINEER.

CIVIL ENGINEER'S OFFICE,
U. S. NAVY-YARD,
Norfolk, Va., March 25, 1890.

SIR: A joint resolution having passed the House of Representatives on the 17th instant calling upon you for a report as to "the advisability, practicability, and approximate cost of tunneling the Detroit River at or near Detroit, Mich., in such a manner as to accommodate the large trade and commerce crossing the river at that point without permanent obstruction of any kind whatsoever to the navigation interests of said river," etc., I respectfully submit the inclosed drawings and description thereof illustrating a system upon which I have devoted much time and study, and which is now before the Michigan Central Railroad undergoing examination.

I will be very much obliged if the plans and description be referred to the Board of Army Engineers mentioned in the resolution referred to.

I will also be much obliged if I may be informed as to what officers constitute the board.

Very respectfully, your obedient servant,

U. S. G. WHITE,
*Civil Engineer, U. S. N.*

Hon. REDFIELD PROCTOR,
*Secretary of War.*

DESCRIPTION OF A SUBMERGED VIADUCT DESIGNED TO AFFORD A PASSAGE ACROSS THE DETROIT RIVER AT DETROIT, MICH.

CIVIL ENGINEER'S OFFICE,
*U. S. Navy-Yard, Norfolk, Va.*

Fig. 1 is a section of the river showing the viaduct.

Fig. 2 is a section at right angles to the axis of the viaduct.

Fig. 3 shows another mode of construction where it is necessary to partly sink the viaduct below the bed of the river to avoid obstructing the stream.

The navigable depth of any river is fixed by the depth at its shallowest point. That of the Detroit River is fixed by the depth at Lime Kiln Crossing (20 feet). This depth was secured by the expenditure of a large amount of money by the United States Government.

An examination of Fig. 1 will show a depth over the viaduct of 21 feet 6 inches. At all stages of the water there will be 18 inches more water over the viaduct than at the Lime Kiln Crossing.

The method of construction is as follows: Rows of piles are driven to which are secured transverse and longitudinal stringers, below and about which is placed a bed of concrete, upon this bed are laid heavy cast-iron plates, these plates are firmly secured to the prepared bed; the cast-iron plates forming the arch are then put together in sections and lowered down to place and firmly secured to the bottom plates by divers. The spaces between the sections are then wedged with soft wood. Upon reaching the shallow water at either bank a coffer-dam is constructed and the approaches are run therefrom. After the coffer-dams are completed the water in the viaduct is pumped out and everything is then in condition for the road-bed and tracks.

The drawings show wooden piles and stringers; in practice iron screw piles and iron stringers would be used, as their holding down power is so much greater. The bed must of necessity be very heavy in order that it may overcome the buoyant effort of the water upon the viaduct.

My calculations of weight and estimates of cost are based upon a thickness of 2 inches for the castings forming the arch.

An examination of the hydrographic chart of the Detroit River shows a section nearly east and west about a mile and a half below the Michigan Central depot which has a depth of 39 feet throughout almost its entire length, this line is about 2,200 feet long with excellent banks through which to construct the approaches.

Estimates based on such information as I have at hand give about one and a quarter millions dollars as the cost of a double-track viaduct on piles. These estimates are only approximate and as I made very liberal allowances for every item I think that estimates made after a careful and complete survey would be considerably less.

Of the practicability of constructing this work I have no doubt. I am convinced that this plan offers the best and most economical means of crossing the river and it will not present any obstruction to the navigation interests of the river.

The only thing to fear is injury from heavy anchors falling upon the arch, this can readily be avoided by having anchorage limits above and below as now obtains where telegraph and other cables cross navigable streams.

I will be very happy to answer any questions or give any further information that may be wanted.

Very respectfully, your obedient servant,

U. S. G. WHITE,
*Civil Engineer, U. S. Navy.*

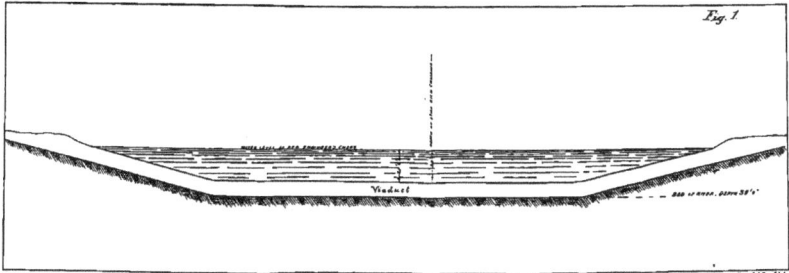

*Fig. 1*

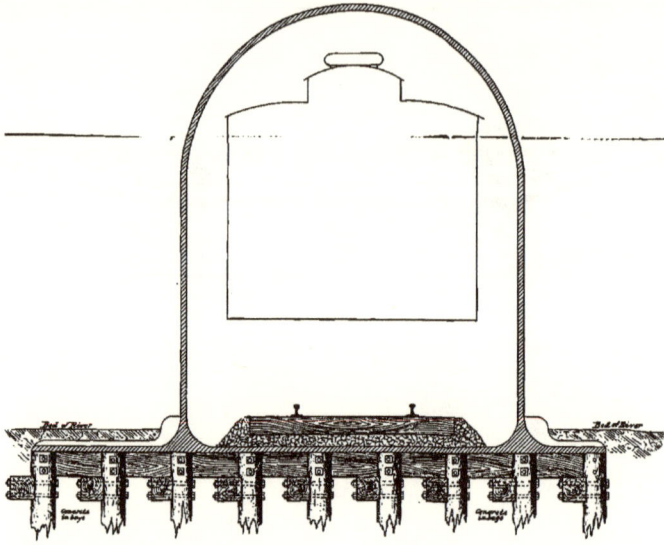

Bed of River                                                    Bed of River

Concrete in Bags          Concrete in Bags

H. S. E. White ..... Civ. Eng.

## D.

### LETTER OF L. GROVER.

HOMER, MICH., *April* 18, 1890.

Honorable SIR: Being interested in Detroit River Tunnel projects, permit me to ask what, if any, control has the War Department over the tunneling of the Detroit River, and what, if any, legislation is now going on in reference to the same? Does a corps of engineers of the War Department sit as a supervising board for the purpose of securing and determining the best plans for its construction? If so, what are the rules or regulations under which they are submitted? What advantage, if any, is gained by the submitting of plans? If any thing is to be gained, I have some very clever plans for a tunnel and tunnel machinery which I would like to submit before the Department makes its report, etc. Would like to know something of the nature of those plans that are before the board, etc. Any information you may be pleased to give will be very gratefully received.

Very respectfully,

L. GROVER.

The SECRETARY OF WAR,
*War Department.*

---

## E.

### LETTER OF MR. CHARLES H. BUCKELEW.

PLAINFIELD, N. J., *April* 29, 1890.

DEAR SIR: The attention of railroad and civil engineers, and all others interested in the construction of submarine tunnels, is called to an improved mode of construction designed by Charles H. Buckelow, of Plainfield, N. J. There has been much difficulty in construction of tunnels hitherto where the soil or mud extended to any great distance below the bed of a river, as the water has a tendency to force its way through the mud unless the tunnel is laid at so great a depth below the bed of a river as to make a very heavy grade or very long approaches to the tunnel.

The plan to which your attention is now called is to construct a tunnel of iron or steel plate of the full size required, and of a proper thickness to withstand the effect of corrosion and wear and tear of the trains to be run through it. The inside may either be left without lining and be painted, or may be lined with cement or brick. The tunnel will be perfectly smooth inside. For a tunnel for a double-track railroad there would be two cylinders of about 18 feet diameter inside, set within a ballast tank large enough to contain the cylinders and ballast enough to sink them. Within the ballast tanks there would be a coating of cement concrete which would entirely surround and encase the tunnel cylinders and *absolutely prevent any corrosion from the outside.* This would be applied before launching the section. The remainder of the ballast tank would be filled up when required to sink the section to the bottom of the river. This tunnel is to be built in sections of proper length (or as long as can be conveniently handled) on the shore and fitted with temporary removable bulkheads at each end (these bulkheads are so arranged that they do not interfere with the fastening of the sections together). On the outsides of the tunnel are placed tanks extending the whole length, on each side, open at the top, and which serve the double purpose of strengthening the sides and keeping them in their proper shape, and also serve as ballast tanks to sink the sections when in position over the trench which has been prepared for its reception. After the section is completed it is launched and towed to the position where it is to be placed, and then either the sections can be lowered separately and then bolted together, or a portion of the bolts can be put in before lowering (which can always be done when the current is not too strong), and after the shore ends are secured in their proper places the bulkheads can be taken out of the sections and the tunnel can either be covered up with mud or left for the mud of the river bottom to fill in around it by the action of the current, which it will do in a short time. The tunnel is then ready for immediate use.

*The joint.*—The mode of joining the sections together is the most important part of this plan, as no diving bells or coffer-dams are required, and the whole tunnel may be put together without any person engaged in its construction running any risk or danger from drowning, or from working in compressed air, as the ventilation in each section can be made perfect, and *all* the work is done from the inside of the section and *no* water is admitted. The joint is made of cast iron or steel; the bolt-holes are all drilled to a template so as to match each other. A blank joint of rubber is then

drawn tight over the holes in such a manner as to exclude the water, and also form
the joint around the bolts when together. This rubber is bolted at its edges in such
manner that the bolts (which are made with long, sharp points) can be driven
through the blank joint without admitting the water around the bolt; at the outside of the line of rubber of the joint another joint is formed by means of a roll of
lead, or other soft material, which will prevent any water passing in to the line of
bolts. After the bolts are permanently screwed up, a recess, which is provided in
the joint, is filled with hydraulic cement, and the joint is then complete.

This plan has peculiar advantages where the river-bottom is soft mud or earth, as
the trench can easily be excavated from the surface, and also has the advantage that
the top of the tunnel can be placed level with the bottom of the river, thus making
the smallest possible grade for the road-bed.

The expense of building a tunnel on this plan with the present low price of iron
would be less than a draw-bridge, and when completed will require no repairs for a
great many years, while the draw-bridge is a constant expense and annoyance.

(The joints and flanges are so arranged that they do not project into the inside of
the tunnel, but will be flush with the inside.)

Entrance to the tunnel while being lowered is by means of a man-hole at the top of
the joint, to which is temporarily fastened a tube of sufficient dimensions for any person to pass up or down on a ladder placed therein.

On the top and end of the adjoining section which is to be lowered there are placed
overlapping sheets or guides which will extend on each side and beyond the man-
hole tube of the section already down, and which will also prevent the descending
section from passing beyond its proper position when down.

It is not necessary that the bed or channel which is dug for the tunnel should be
leveled off or made solid on the bottom, as there is sufficient strength in the tunnel
itself to hold itself in position after the shore ends are secured in their proper place
until the proper filling of mud or sand can be dropped down in such position that it
will settle underneath and around the tunnel.

It is to be remembered that this tunnel *does not weigh anything in the water*, and
therefore the weight of the trains only have to be provided for on the bed.

For further information address,

CHARLES H. BUCKELEW,<br>
10 *West Fifth Street, Plainfield, N. J.*

The best possible mode of crossing the Detroit River, see H. R. Bill 119.
Hon. SECRETARY OF WAR.

---

## F.

LETTER OF MR. R. P. ROTHWELL.

THE ENGINEERING AND MINING JOURNAL,<br>
*New York, U. S. A., April* 30, 1890.

GENTLEMEN: I notice that you have been appointed a board to report upon the
practicability and estimated cost of the proposed Detroit River tunnel. I would
very much like to call your attention to the Hall method of tunneling, which presents
great advantages over the method now being used at Port Huron and in fact covers
with patents the method there called the "Greathead system."

I would very much like to show you the plans and estimates for the Detroit River
tunnel made by Mr. Hall, and which I have examined myself. I think they would
interest you and perhaps be of assistance in making your report.

Yours, truly,

R. P. ROTHWELL.

Colonel POE or Captain ALLEN or Captain ADAMS,
*of the United States Engineers.*